DISNEY
PRINCESS
MAD LIBS®

by Sarah Fabiny

MAD LIBS

An Imprint of Penguin Random House LLC, New York

Mad Libs format copyright © 2019 by Penguin Random House LLC.
All rights reserved.

Concept created by Roger Price & Leonard Stern

Copyright © 2019 Disney Enterprises, Inc. All rights reserved.

Published by Mad Libs,
an imprint of Penguin Random House LLC, New York.
Printed in the USA.

Visit us online at www.penguinrandomhouse.com.

Penguin supports copyright. Copyright fuels creativity, encourages diverse voices, promotes free speech, and creates a vibrant culture. Thank you for buying an authorized edition of this book and for complying with copyright laws by not reproducing, scanning, or distributing any part of it in any form without permission. You are supporting writers and allowing Penguin to continue to publish books for every reader.

ISBN 9780593093924
3 5 7 9 10 8 6 4

MAD LIBS is a registered trademark of Penguin Random House LLC.

INSTRUCTIONS

MAD LIBS® is a game for people who don't like games!
It can be played by one, two, three, four, or forty.

• RIDICULOUSLY SIMPLE DIRECTIONS

In this tablet you will find stories containing blank spaces where words are left out. One player, the READER, selects one of these stories. The READER does not tell anyone what the story is about. Instead, he/she asks the other players, the WRITERS, to give him/her words. These words are used to fill in the blank spaces in the story.

• TO PLAY

The READER asks each WRITER in turn to call out a word—an adjective or a noun or whatever the space calls for—and uses them to fill in the blank spaces in the story. The result is a MAD LIBS® game.

When the READER then reads the completed MAD LIBS® game to the other players, they will discover that they have written a story that is fantastic, screamingly funny, shocking, silly, crazy, or just plain dumb—depending upon which words each WRITER called out.

• EXAMPLE (*Before* and *After*)

"_____!" he said _____
      EXCLAMATION   ADVERB

as he jumped into his convertible _____ and
                                        NOUN

drove off with his _____ wife.
                    ADJECTIVE

"_____OUCH_____!" he said _____HAPPILY_____
      EXCLAMATION   ADVERB

as he jumped into his convertible _____CAT_____ and
                                          NOUN

drove off with his _____BRAVE_____ wife.
                    ADJECTIVE

QUICK REVIEW

In case you have forgotten what adjectives, adverbs, nouns, and verbs are, here is a quick review:

An ADJECTIVE describes something or somebody. *Lumpy, soft, ugly, messy,* and *short* are adjectives.

An ADVERB tells how something is done. It modifies a verb and usually ends in "ly." *Modestly, stupidly, greedily,* and *carefully* are adverbs.

A NOUN is the name of a person, place, or thing. *Sidewalk, umbrella, bridle, bathtub,* and *nose* are nouns.

A VERB is an action word. *Run, pitch, jump,* and *swim* are verbs. Put the verbs in past tense if the directions say PAST TENSE. *Ran, pitched, jumped,* and *swam* are verbs in the past tense.

When we ask for A PLACE, we mean any sort of place: a country or city *(Spain, Cleveland)* or a room *(bathroom, kitchen).*

An EXCLAMATION or SILLY WORD is any sort of funny sound, gasp, grunt, or outcry, like *Wow!, Ouch!, Whomp!, Ick!,* and *Gadzooks!*

When we ask for specific words, like a NUMBER, a COLOR, an ANIMAL, or a PART OF THE BODY, we mean a word that is one of those things, like *seven, blue, horse,* or *head.*

When we ask for a PLURAL, it means more than one. For example, *cat* pluralized is *cats.*

MAD LIBS® is fun to play with friends, but you can also play it by yourself! To begin with, DO NOT look at the story on the page below. Fill in the blanks on this page with the words called for. Then, using the words you have selected, fill in the blank spaces in the story.

Now you've created your own hilarious MAD LIBS® game!

TIANA'S PALACE MENU

NOUN _____

NOUN _____

ADJECTIVE _____

ADJECTIVE _____

TYPE OF FOOD (PLURAL) _____

PLURAL NOUN _____

ADJECTIVE _____

ADJECTIVE _____

PLURAL NOUN _____

ADJECTIVE _____

ADJECTIVE _____

TYPE OF FOOD _____

NOUN _____

ADJECTIVE _____

NOUN _____

Welcome to Tiana's Palace—the restaurant with the best _____

NOUN

in New Orleans! Take a look at our _____. We're sure you'll

NOUN

find something _____ to eat!

ADJECTIVE

APPETIZERS

- Louisiana _____ Crab Dip with Toasted _____

ADJECTIVE TYPE OF FOOD (PLURAL)
- Sautéed Gulf Shrimp and _____ with _____

PLURAL NOUN ADJECTIVE

  Barbecue Sauce

ENTRÉES

- _____ Shrimp with Cajun _____ and _____ Rice

ADJECTIVE PLURAL NOUN ADJECTIVE
- Big Daddy's _____ Prime Rib with a Double-Baked _____

ADJECTIVE TYPE OF FOOD

DESSERTS

- Mama Odie's _____ Pudding with _____ Sauce

NOUN ADJECTIVE
- Tiana's Buttermilk Beignets dusted with Powdered _____

NOUN

Bon appétit!

From DISNEY PRINCESS MAD LIBS® • Copyright © 2019 Disney Enterprises, Inc. All rights reserved.
Published by Mad Libs, an imprint of Penguin Random House LLC.

MAD LIBS® is fun to play with friends, but you can also play it by yourself! To begin with, DO NOT look at the story on the page below. Fill in the blanks on this page with the words called for. Then, using the words you have selected, fill in the blank spaces in the story.

Now you've created your own hilarious MAD LIBS® game!

SO YOU WANT HAIR LIKE RAPUNZEL'S?

NOUN _____

ADJECTIVE _____

NUMBER _____

VERB ENDING IN "ING" _____

PLURAL NOUN _____

ADJECTIVE _____

ANIMAL _____

VERB _____

SAME VERB _____

NUMBER _____

NOUN _____

ADJECTIVE _____

ADJECTIVE _____

VERB _____

PLURAL NOUN _____

ADJECTIVE _____

MAD LIBS®
SO YOU WANT HAIR LIKE RAPUNZEL'S?

Even though you may be trapped in a secluded _____ , it's still
                                            NOUN

important to look after your hair. Especially when it's _____ ,
                                                         ADJECTIVE

_____ feet long, and has _____ powers. So here
  NUMBER   VERB ENDING IN "ING"

are some important hints and _____ :
                              PLURAL NOUN

• Use a/an _____ hairbrush. A/An _____-bristle
             ADJECTIVE   ANIMAL

brush will be your best friend.

• Don't _____ your hair every day. To keep your hair healthy,
          VERB

you only need to _____ it two to _____ times a week.
                  SAME VERB   NUMBER

• Only use a/an _____ -size amount of shampoo, and
                  NOUN

be _____ .
     ADJECTIVE

• Use a/an _____ conditioner. This will _____
             ADJECTIVE   VERB

moisture into your hair.

Follow these easy _____ to ensure that your hair will always
                   PLURAL NOUN

be healthy and _____ , just like Rapunzel's.
                 ADJECTIVE

From DISNEY PRINCESS MAD LIBS® • Copyright © 2019 Disney Enterprises, Inc. All rights reserved.
Published by Mad Libs, an imprint of Penguin Random House LLC.

MAD LIBS® is fun to play with friends, but you can also play it by yourself! To begin with, DO NOT look at the story on the page below. Fill in the blanks on this page with the words called for. Then, using the words you have selected, fill in the blank spaces in the story.

Now you've created your own hilarious MAD LIBS® game!

BELLE'S FAVORITE BOOKS

ANIMAL _____

VERB ENDING IN "ING" _____

PERSON IN ROOM_____

NOUN _____

PERSON IN ROOM_____

ADJECTIVE _____

PLURAL NOUN _____

NUMBER _____

PLURAL NOUN _____

PERSON IN ROOM_____

NOUN _____

VERB _____

VERB _____

ADJECTIVE _____

MAD LIBS®

BELLE'S FAVORITE BOOKS

People are always teasing me about being a book-_____ . But I
                                                    ANIMAL

love nothing more than _____ books. And here are
                        VERB ENDING IN "ING"

some of my favorites:

- _____ **and the Beanstalk**: an exciting tale about a
  PERSON IN ROOM

  beanstalk and a/an _____
                      NOUN

- **Romeo and** _____ : a/an _____ story
                PERSON IN ROOM   ADJECTIVE

  about two _____ in fair Verona
            PLURAL NOUN

- **The** _____ **Musketeers:** an adventure story with sword fights
          NUMBER

  and _____
      PLURAL NOUN

- **King** _____ **and the Knights of the Round** _____ :
           PERSON IN ROOM   NOUN

  an epic saga and the perfect book to _____ aloud
                                        VERB

No matter what you like to _____ , you'll never be alone with a/an
                            VERB

_____ book!
 ADJECTIVE

From DISNEY PRINCESS MAD LIBS® • Copyright © 2019 Disney Enterprises, Inc. All rights reserved.
Published by Mad Libs, an imprint of Penguin Random House LLC.

MAD LIBS® is fun to play with friends, but you can also play it by yourself! To begin with, DO NOT look at the story on the page below. Fill in the blanks on this page with the words called for. Then, using the words you have selected, fill in the blank spaces in the story.

Now you've created your own hilarious MAD LIBS® game!

LIFE IS AN ADVENTURE
WITH POCAHONTAS

VERB _____

ADJECTIVE _____

ADJECTIVE _____

NOUN _____

ADJECTIVE _____

NOUN _____

ADJECTIVE _____

ADJECTIVE _____

NOUN _____

VERB _____

NOUN _____

ADJECTIVE _____

NOUN _____

VERB _____

NOUN _____

ADJECTIVE _____

COLOR _____

Pocahontas: Good morning, Nakoma! What shall we _____ today?
                                                              VERB

Nakoma: Hi, Pocahontas. Let's make it a great morning and do something

_____ .
   ADJECTIVE

Pocahontas: I was thinking we'd do something _____! What if
                                                      ADJECTIVE

we jump in a/an _____ and take a trip down the river today?
                    NOUN

Nakoma: A trip down the river would be _____, as long as
                                               ADJECTIVE

you promise not to dive off the _____ again.
                                     NOUN

Pocahontas: Diving into the water is _____! And I'm so good at it!
                                            ADJECTIVE

Nakoma: Well, it's a little too _____ for me. How about
                                         ADJECTIVE

taking a quiet _____ through the forest?
                    NOUN

Pocahontas: Or we could _____ through the forest!
                                 VERB

Nakoma: What if I trip on a/an _____? Why can't we just
                                        NOUN

do something _____ for once?
                 ADJECTIVE

Pocahontas: Oh, Nakoma! You are my best _____, but you
                                                  NOUN

_____ too much! Life is meant to be a/an _____!
   VERB   NOUN

Nakoma: And you are my _____ friend, but you are going to
                                ADJECTIVE

give me _____ hair.
             COLOR

From DISNEY PRINCESS MAD LIBS® • Copyright © 2019 Disney Enterprises, Inc. All rights reserved.
Published by Mad Libs, an imprint of Penguin Random House LLC.

MAD LIBS® is fun to play with friends, but you can also play it by yourself! To begin with, DO NOT look at the story on the page below. Fill in the blanks on this page with the words called for. Then, using the words you have selected, fill in the blank spaces in the story.

Now you've created your own hilarious MAD LIBS® game!

ARIEL'S TREASURES

VERB ENDING IN "ING" _____

ADJECTIVE _____

PLURAL NOUN _____

PLURAL NOUN _____

A PLACE _____

PLURAL NOUN _____

ADJECTIVE _____

NOUN _____

A PLACE _____

ADJECTIVE _____

ADJECTIVE _____

PLURAL NOUN _____

COLOR _____

PLURAL NOUN _____

ANIMAL _____

ADJECTIVE _____

NOUN _____

COLOR _____

MAD LIBS®
ARIEL'S TREASURES

Ariel loves _____ treasures for her _____
         VERB ENDING IN "ING"   ADJECTIVE

grotto. It's full of _____ and gizmos, _____ and whatsits—
              PLURAL NOUN   PLURAL NOUN

she's got everything under (the) _____. Ariel explores places like
                                    A PLACE

sunken _____ and _____ caves for her treasures.
         PLURAL NOUN   ADJECTIVE

After she's found something special, she puts it in her _____
                                                              NOUN

and then brings it back to her _____ to store with the rest of
                                   A PLACE

her collection.

Here are some of the _____ thingamabobs she's collected:
                          ADJECTIVE

• _____ candelabras
        ADJECTIVE

• Musical _____
            PLURAL NOUN

• _____ jewelry made of rubies and _____
        COLOR   PLURAL NOUN

• A/An _____ -cage
          ANIMAL

But Ariel's most _____ treasure is a dinglehopper (otherwise
                      ADJECTIVE

known as a/an _____). Everyone knows that a dinglehopper
                   NOUN

should only be used to comb your luscious _____ hair.
                                                COLOR

From DISNEY PRINCESS MAD LIBS® • Copyright © 2019 Disney Enterprises, Inc. All rights reserved.
Published by Mad Libs, an imprint of Penguin Random House LLC.

MAD LIBS® is fun to play with friends, but you can also play it by yourself! To begin with, DO NOT look at the story on the page below. Fill in the blanks on this page with the words called for. Then, using the words you have selected, fill in the blank spaces in the story.

Now you've created your own hilarious MAD LIBS® game!

JASMINE'S WISHES

ADJECTIVE _____

ADJECTIVE _____

NUMBER _____

VERB _____

VERB ENDING IN "ING" _____

NOUN _____

A PLACE _____

PLURAL NOUN _____

ADJECTIVE _____

ANIMAL (PLURAL) _____

VERB _____

NOUN _____

ADJECTIVE _____

TYPE OF FOOD _____

ADJECTIVE _____

NOUN _____

MAD LIBS®

JASMINE'S WISHES

I love my life in Agrabah, and I am very _____ , but sometimes

ADJECTIVE

I wish I could find a/an _____ lamp to grant me wishes. I hope

ADJECTIVE

I'd get more than _____ wishes! There are so many things I would

NUMBER

_____ for. Instead of _____ on a magic carpet,

VERB   VERB ENDING IN "ING"

I think it would be better to ride on a magic _____ . Aladdin

NOUN

and I traveled to China to see beautiful fireworks, but I'd also love to travel to

(the) _____ to see _____! I love Rajah, my

A PLACE   PLURAL NOUN

_____ pet tiger, but it would be fun to have some cats, dogs, and

ADJECTIVE

pet _____ in the palace, too. Most importantly, I know I could

ANIMAL (PLURAL)

_____ wishes to help the people of Agrabah! I could wish for

VERB

a/an _____ so all the kids in the city could have a place to play.

NOUN

And how wonderful would it be to wish for a/an _____ feast for all

ADJECTIVE

of Agrabah to eat _____ and be _____! I better

TYPE OF FOOD   ADJECTIVE

start searching for a golden _____!

NOUN

From DISNEY PRINCESS MAD LIBS® • Copyright © 2019 Disney Enterprises, Inc. All rights reserved.
Published by Mad Libs, an imprint of Penguin Random House LLC.

MAD LIBS® is fun to play with friends, but you can also play it by yourself! To begin with, DO NOT look at the story on the page below. Fill in the blanks on this page with the words called for. Then, using the words you have selected, fill in the blank spaces in the story.

Now you've created your own hilarious MAD LIBS® game!

SNOW WHITE'S SEVEN FRIENDS

VERB _____

ADJECTIVE _____

VERB _____

ADJECTIVE _____

PLURAL NOUN _____

ADJECTIVE _____

VERB _____

ANIMAL _____

ADJECTIVE _____

COLOR _____

ADJECTIVE _____

PLURAL NOUN _____

NOUN _____

VERB ENDING IN "ING" _____

COLOR _____

The seven dwarfs are the best friends anyone could _____ for!
VERB

They are all _____ for very different reasons:
ADJECTIVE

- **Sleepy** is always very tired, which means he tends to _____ a
VERB

  bit slower than the rest.

- **Doc** is rational, organized, and _____ . But sometimes **he**
ADJECTIVE

  mixes up his _____ .
PLURAL NOUN

- **Dopey** is playful and _____ ! No one has ever **heard him**
ADJECTIVE

  _____ . He's as quiet as a/an _____ .
VERB   ANIMAL

- **Bashful** is the most _____ of the dwarfs, which means his **face**
ADJECTIVE

  is always turning _____ .
COLOR

- **Sneezy** is friendly, but his _____ sneezes will blow you **away!**
ADJECTIVE

- **Happy** is the friendliest of the _____ and will welcome **anyone**
PLURAL NOUN

  into their _____ .
NOUN

- **Grumpy** may always be _____ , but he really does **have a**
VERB ENDING IN "ING"

  heart of _____ .
COLOR

From DISNEY PRINCESS MAD LIBS® • Copyright © 2019 Disney Enterprises, Inc. All rights reserved.
Published by Mad Libs, an imprint of Penguin Random House LLC.

MAD LIBS® is fun to play with friends, but you can also play it by yourself! To begin with, DO NOT look at the story on the page below. Fill in the blanks on this page with the words called for. Then, using the words you have selected, fill in the blank spaces in the story.

Now you've created your own hilarious MAD LIBS® game!

CINDERELLA'S FAVORITE SHOES

NOUN _____

PLURAL NOUN _____

ADJECTIVE _____

VERB ENDING IN "ING" _____

PLURAL NOUN _____

NOUN _____

NOUN _____

PERSON IN ROOM _____

ADJECTIVE _____

PLURAL NOUN _____

ADJECTIVE _____

VERB ENDING IN "ING" _____

VERB _____

As they say, a/an _____ can never have too many pairs of shoes.
NOUN

Now, I personally don't have a lot of footwear, but the _____ I
PLURAL NOUN

do have all come in handy. For example, I have a/an _____ pair
ADJECTIVE

of flats that are perfect to wear when I'm _____ by the
VERB ENDING IN "ING"

fireplace, mending _____, or cooking a delicious _____.
PLURAL NOUN   NOUN

I also have a sturdy pair of clogs made of _____. I wear them
NOUN

when _____ and I go for _____ walks through
PERSON IN ROOM   ADJECTIVE

town—they're very fashionable. But, of course, my favorite shoes are glass

_____. They were an extra-special gift from my _____
PLURAL NOUN   ADJECTIVE

godmother and are perfect for _____ till midnight at a
VERB ENDING IN "ING"

ball. Just make sure you don't _____ one on your way home!
VERB

From DISNEY PRINCESS MAD LIBS® • Copyright © 2019 Disney Enterprises, Inc. All rights reserved.
Published by Mad Libs, an imprint of Penguin Random House LLC.

MAD LIBS® is fun to play with friends, but you can also play it by yourself! To begin with, DO NOT look at the story on the page below. Fill in the blanks on this page with the words called for. Then, using the words you have selected, fill in the blank spaces in the story.

Now you've created your own hilarious MAD LIBS® game!

AURORA'S BIRTHDAY SURPRISE

NOUN _____

NUMBER _____

ADJECTIVE _____

ADJECTIVE _____

PLURAL NOUN _____

ADJECTIVE _____

ADJECTIVE _____

VERB _____

PLURAL NOUN _____

EXCLAMATION _____

PLURAL NOUN _____

PERSON IN ROOM _____

NOUN _____

NOUN _____

Flora: Happy birthday, Briar _____! Today is your birthday and

NOUN

you are _____ years old.

NUMBER

Fauna: You have grown into such a/an _____ young woman.

ADJECTIVE

Merryweather: But there are some _____ things we need to tell you.

ADJECTIVE

Briar Rose: Is this about what _____ you got for my birthday?

PLURAL NOUN

Flora: No, nothing as _____ as that. We're afraid our news is a bit

ADJECTIVE

more _____.

ADJECTIVE

Merryweather: First we need to _____ you that we are not your

VERB

aunties. We are actually three good _____.

PLURAL NOUN

Briar Rose: _____! How can that be?

EXCLAMATION

Fauna: We may look like ordinary women, but we have secret magical

_____. And your real name isn't _____. It is Aurora.

PLURAL NOUN   _PERSON IN ROOM_

Briar Rose: Aurora?

Merryweather: Yes, your parents, the _____ and queen, named

NOUN

you after the light of the dawn.

Briar Rose: If my parents are royal . . . does that mean I am a . . .

Flora: Yes, my darling, you are a/an _____!

NOUN

From DISNEY PRINCESS MAD LIBS® • Copyright © 2019 Disney Enterprises, Inc. All rights reserved.
Published by Mad Libs, an imprint of Penguin Random House LLC.

MAD LIBS® is fun to play with friends, but you can also play it by yourself! To begin with, DO NOT look at the story on the page below. Fill in the blanks on this page with the words called for. Then, using the words you have selected, fill in the blank spaces in the story.

Now you've created your own hilarious MAD LIBS® game!

IS YOUR MOTHER A BEAR?
BY MERIDA

ADJECTIVE _____

ADJECTIVE _____

ADJECTIVE _____

ARTICLE OF CLOTHING _____

ADJECTIVE _____

PART OF THE BODY _____

ADJECTIVE _____

PLURAL NOUN _____

ADJECTIVE _____

VERB ENDING IN "ING" _____

ANIMAL (PLURAL) _____

PLURAL NOUN _____

VERB ENDING IN "ING" _____

ANIMAL _____

ADJECTIVE _____

ADJECTIVE _____

EXCLAMATION _____

Here is a/an _____ quiz to determine if your mother has been
ADJECTIVE

turned into a bear.

1. Instead of long, _____ brown hair, she . . .
ADJECTIVE

(a) now has _____ blond hair
ADJECTIVE

(b) is now wearing a pink _____
ARTICLE OF CLOTHING

(c) is now covered in _____ brown fur
ADJECTIVE

2. Her _____ have been replaced by . . .
PART OF THE BODY

(a) _____ , slippery fins
ADJECTIVE

(b) long wings covered in _____
PLURAL NOUN

(c) huge paws with _____ claws
ADJECTIVE

3. Instead of _____ with a Scottish accent, she is now . . .
VERB ENDING IN "ING"

(a) barking and chasing _____
ANIMAL (PLURAL)

(b) chirping and building a nest from _____
PLURAL NOUN

(c) growling and _____ small critters
VERB ENDING IN "ING"

4. Your mother now sleeps . . .

(a) in a cute _____ -house
ANIMAL

(b) on a/an _____ purple pillow
ADJECTIVE

(c) in a/an _____ , dark cave
ADJECTIVE

If you answered *c* to any of these questions— _____ ! Your
EXCLAMATION

mother is a bear.

From DISNEY PRINCESS MAD LIBS® • Copyright © 2019 Disney Enterprises, Inc. All rights reserved.
Published by Mad Libs, an imprint of Penguin Random House LLC.

MAD LIBS® is fun to play with friends, but you can also play it by yourself! To begin with, DO NOT look at the story on the page below. Fill in the blanks on this page with the words called for. Then, using the words you have selected, fill in the blank spaces in the story.

Now you've created your own hilarious MAD LIBS® game!

HOW TO LOOK AFTER A TIGER, BY JASMINE

ADJECTIVE _____

ANIMAL _____

COLOR _____

ADJECTIVE _____

NOUN _____

VERB ENDING IN "ING" _____

NUMBER _____

PLURAL NOUN _____

ADJECTIVE _____

VERB _____

ADJECTIVE _____

VERB _____

TYPE OF FOOD _____

ADJECTIVE _____

VERB _____

ADJECTIVE _____

VERB ENDING IN "ING" _____

Maybe you have a/an _____ dog, a cuddly _____,
ADJECTIVE   ANIMAL

or a rabbit with a cute _____ nose as a pet. But my pet is a big
COLOR

_____ tiger named Rajah. And he isn't just my pet; he is my
ADJECTIVE

very best _____. But _____ for Rajah can be a
NOUN   VERB ENDING IN "ING"

whole lot of work. He's over _____ pounds and more than eleven
NUMBER

_____ long. Here are some _____ rules for raising a
PLURAL NOUN   ADJECTIVE

pet tiger:

• Tigers need a lot of space where they can jump, climb, and _____.
VERB

A bored tiger is a/an _____ tiger.
ADJECTIVE

• Tigers like to swim, so make sure you have a big pond or lake they can

_____ around in.
VERB

• Tigers eat _____—and a lot of it. So make sure you have
TYPE OF FOOD

enough food around—a hungry tiger can be _____.
ADJECTIVE

More than anything, tigers love to _____, so make sure they have
VERB

a nice _____ spot where they can rest. I never disturb Rajah when
ADJECTIVE

he is _____!
VERB ENDING IN "ING"

From DISNEY PRINCESS MAD LIBS® • Copyright © 2019 Disney Enterprises, Inc. All rights reserved.
Published by Mad Libs, an imprint of Penguin Random House LLC.

MAD LIBS® is fun to play with friends, but you can also play it by yourself! To begin with, DO NOT look at the story on the page below. Fill in the blanks on this page with the words called for. Then, using the words you have selected, fill in the blank spaces in the story.

Now you've created your own hilarious MAD LIBS® game!

THE WORK OF A FAIRY GODMOTHER IS NEVER DONE

SILLY WORD _____

NOUN _____

ADJECTIVE _____

NOUN _____

NOUN _____

ADJECTIVE _____

PLURAL NOUN _____

ADJECTIVE _____

NOUN _____

ADJECTIVE _____

NOUN _____

EXCLAMATION _____

NOUN _____

ADJECTIVE _____

SILLY WORD _____

SILLY WORD _____

VERB ENDING IN "ING" _____

VERB _____

Oh, _____! Fairy Godmother here. What have I done with my
_____SILLY WORD_____

magic _____? Without it, I won't be able to get Cinderella ready
_____NOUN_____

for the ball! I have some _____ tricks up my _____
_____ADJECTIVE_____   _____NOUN_____

to help her stand out. Once I find my _____, I'll change an
_____NOUN_____

ordinary pumpkin into a/an _____ carriage! I'll turn squeaky
_____ADJECTIVE_____

mice into beautiful, dashing _____. And of course, I'll use
_____PLURAL NOUN_____

my _____ wand to transform Cinderella's _____ into
_____ADJECTIVE_____   _____NOUN_____

a/an _____ gown! She'll be the _____ of the ball!
_____ADJECTIVE_____   _____NOUN_____

_____! I found my magic _____. But now I have
_____EXCLAMATION_____   _____NOUN_____

to remember my _____ word. Is it _____? Or
_____ADJECTIVE_____   _____SILLY WORD_____

_____? Oh, of course, it's "bibbidi-bobbidi-boo"! Oh, I hear
_____SILLY WORD_____

Cinderella _____! Time for me to go _____
_____VERB ENDING IN "ING"_____   _____VERB_____

some magic!

From DISNEY PRINCESS MAD LIBS® • Copyright © 2019 Disney Enterprises, Inc. All rights reserved.
Published by Mad Libs, an imprint of Penguin Random House LLC.

MAD LIBS® is fun to play with friends, but you can also play it by yourself! To begin with, DO NOT look at the story on the page below. Fill in the blanks on this page with the words called for. Then, using the words you have selected, fill in the blank spaces in the story.

Now you've created your own hilarious MAD LIBS® game!

GIRL POWER! WITH MULAN

PLURAL NOUN _____

VERB _____

PLURAL NOUN _____

VERB ENDING IN "ING" _____

NOUN _____

PLURAL NOUN _____

ADJECTIVE _____

NOUN _____

NOUN _____

ANIMAL _____

NOUN _____

SAME NOUN _____

NOUN _____

VERB _____

PLURAL NOUN _____

ANIMAL _____

NOUN _____

ADJECTIVE _____

Lots of _____ from my village say a girl shouldn't _____
             PLURAL NOUN   VERB

the army, but girls can do anything as well as _____—that's
                                                    PLURAL NOUN

what makes us equal! _____ for your country is about
                       VERB ENDING IN "ING"

bravery and _____, and those qualities can be found inside
                  NOUN

anyone! We all have special _____ that make us unique and
                                PLURAL NOUN

stronger as a team. For example, I love to show off my _____ skills
                                                           ADJECTIVE

in archery. I can shoot a/an _____ as fast as any _____
                                 NOUN   NOUN

can. And I hit the _____'s-eye. Every time. Not to brag, but
                        ANIMAL

I'm also great with a/an _____. People say it's too heavy for girls
                             NOUN

to pick up, but just watch me swing that _____. Stand back!
                                             SAME NOUN

Anyone can be strong when they put their _____ to it! And
                                             NOUN

sometimes when I'm tired and feel I can't _____ anymore, my
                                              VERB

_____ remind me I'm as strong as a/an _____! So
   PLURAL NOUN   ANIMAL

here's to _____ power and being a/an _____ fighter!
               NOUN   ADJECTIVE

From DISNEY PRINCESS MAD LIBS® • Copyright © 2019 Disney Enterprises, Inc. All rights reserved.
Published by Mad Libs, an imprint of Penguin Random House LLC.

MAD LIBS® is fun to play with friends, but you can also play it by yourself! To begin with, DO NOT look at the story on the page below. Fill in the blanks on this page with the words called for. Then, using the words you have selected, fill in the blank spaces in the story.

Now you've created your own hilarious MAD LIBS® game!

SET SAIL WITH MOANA

NOUN _____

VERB _____

PLURAL NOUN _____

ADJECTIVE _____

VERB _____

NUMBER _____

ADJECTIVE _____

VERB _____

NUMBER _____

PLURAL NOUN _____

ADJECTIVE _____

VERB _____

ADJECTIVE _____

ADJECTIVE _____

NOUN _____

ADJECTIVE _____

ADVERB _____

PART OF THE BODY _____

MAD LIBS

SET SAIL WITH MOANA

I sailed my _____ from Motunui to Te Fiti's island. But there
          NOUN

is so much more to _____ in the world! So follow my
               VERB

_____ and set out on an adventure. You just need to be
  PLURAL NOUN

_____ and brave.
  ADJECTIVE

- You could _____ to the very top of Motunui. It will take
             VERB

  you _____ minutes to climb the _____ steps up the
     NUMBER   ADJECTIVE

  mountain. Don't forget to bring a conch shell to _____ at the top!
                              VERB

- Adventure into a hidden cave that's only _____ steps from the
                          NUMBER

  beach. You'll find ancient _____ and _____ drums
              PLURAL NOUN   ADJECTIVE

  inside!

- You can _____ all the way to the Realm of Monsters if
           VERB

  you're _____ enough. Just watch out for a/an _____
     ADJECTIVE   ADJECTIVE

  crab named Tamatoa. He can be a real _____ .
                           NOUN

- Don't forget that all _____ adventures begin just beyond the reef.
             ADJECTIVE

  Grab a boat, paddle as _____ as you can, and make it to the
              ADVERB

  open ocean!

But no matter how far you go, remember to follow your _____!
                                     PART OF THE BODY

From DISNEY PRINCESS MAD LIBS® • Copyright © 2019 Disney Enterprises, Inc. All rights reserved.
Published by Mad Libs, an imprint of Penguin Random House LLC.

MAD LIBS® is fun to play with friends, but you can also play it by yourself! To begin with, DO NOT look at the story on the page below. Fill in the blanks on this page with the words called for. Then, using the words you have selected, fill in the blank spaces in the story.

Now you've created your own hilarious MAD LIBS® game!

BELLE SEES BEAUTY IN THE BEAST

NOUN _____

NOUN _____

ADJECTIVE _____

ADJECTIVE _____

VERB _____

NOUN _____

A PLACE _____

VERB ENDING IN "ING" _____

ADJECTIVE _____

PLURAL NOUN _____

ADJECTIVE _____

NOUN _____

ADJECTIVE _____

ADJECTIVE _____

ADVERB _____

ADJECTIVE _____

A PLACE _____

PLURAL NOUN _____

I love reading and never judge a book by its _____ . I've also
__NOUN__

learned never to judge a person by their _____ , because looks
__NOUN__

can be _____ . Look at Gaston, for example. He is handsome
__ADJECTIVE__

and _____ . The townspeople _____ him. But he is
__ADJECTIVE__ __VERB__

also arrogant and a big _____ . He's almost never visited (the)
__NOUN__

_____ to borrow a book and thinks _____ is silly!
__A PLACE__ __VERB ENDING IN "ING"__

The townspeople may think my father is a bit _____ , but he is
__ADJECTIVE__

one of the smartest _____ I know. His inventions may be a
__PLURAL NOUN__

little _____ and out of the ordinary, but someday he will invent
__ADJECTIVE__

something that changes our _____ . Most _____ of
__NOUN__ __ADJECTIVE__

all is the Beast. Although he is big and _____ and can roar quite
__ADJECTIVE__

_____ , he is gentle and has a/an _____ heart. He even
__ADVERB__ __ADJECTIVE__

gave me all the books in (the) _____—how kind! Now I have lots
__A PLACE__

of books I won't judge by their _____ .
__PLURAL NOUN__

From DISNEY PRINCESS MAD LIBS® • Copyright © 2019 Disney Enterprises, Inc. All rights reserved.
Published by Mad Libs, an imprint of Penguin Random House LLC.

MAD LIBS® is fun to play with friends, but you can also play it by yourself! To begin with, DO NOT look at the story on the page below. Fill in the blanks on this page with the words called for. Then, using the words you have selected, fill in the blank spaces in the story.

Now you've created your own hilarious MAD LIBS® game!

MERIDA HITS THE BULL'S-EYE!

PLURAL NOUN _____

ADJECTIVE _____

VERB _____

PART OF THE BODY (PLURAL) _____

ADJECTIVE _____

VERB _____

NOUN _____

PART OF THE BODY _____

NOUN _____

ANIMAL _____

NOUN _____

ADJECTIVE _____

ADJECTIVE _____

Here are some basic _____ you can follow if you want to

PLURAL NOUN

become a/an _____ archer like me, Merida.

ADJECTIVE

1. **Stance:** _____ upright with your feet shoulder-width apart

VERB

   and your _____ facing the target.

PART OF THE BODY (PLURAL)

2. **Grip:** Keep a/an _____ grip on the bow handle.

ADJECTIVE

3. **Position:** _____ the arrow on the bow.

VERB

4. **Draw:** Pull back the _____ until it touches the tip of

NOUN

   your nose.

5. **Aim:** Using your dominant _____, look down at the

PART OF THE BODY

   arrow and align it with the _____. Visualize your arrow

NOUN

   hitting the _____'s-eye.

ANIMAL

6. **Release:** Relax your grip and watch the _____ fly toward

NOUN

   the target.

With some _____ practice, you may be able to master archery.

ADJECTIVE

_____ luck!

ADJECTIVE

From DISNEY PRINCESS MAD LIBS® • Copyright © 2019 Disney Enterprises, Inc. All rights reserved.
Published by Mad Libs, an imprint of Penguin Random House LLC.

MAD LIBS® is fun to play with friends, but you can also play it by yourself! To begin with, DO NOT look at the story on the page below. Fill in the blanks on this page with the words called for. Then, using the words you have selected, fill in the blank spaces in the story.

Now you've created your own hilarious MAD LIBS® game!

FIND YOUR INNER WARRIOR WITH MULAN

ADJECTIVE _____

PLURAL NOUN _____

VERB _____

PLURAL NOUN _____

VERB _____

PART OF THE BODY (PLURAL) _____

VERB _____

NUMBER _____

NUMBER _____

VERB _____

NOUN _____

PLURAL NOUN _____

ADJECTIVE _____

PLURAL NOUN _____

ADJECTIVE _____

NOUN _____

NOUN _____

Even though it can be scary—and a bit _____—we all have the
                                            ADJECTIVE

power to rise up to challenges. Each day is full of new _____
                                                          PLURAL NOUN

to learn from to help you _____ into all you want to be. Think
                            VERB

of the magnolia tree. Not all _____ bloom at the same time.
                                PLURAL NOUN

Some flowers take their time to _____, and people are like
                                   VERB

that, too. We all grow at our own pace. Just stay focused and keep your

_____ on the prize. Here's some advice:
PART OF THE BODY (PLURAL)

- It's okay to make mistakes— _____ from them! Fall down
                                VERB

  _____ times, get up _____ .
       NUMBER   NUMBER

- _____ out of your comfort zone. A little _____ can
      VERB   NOUN

  go a long way.

- Celebrate all your _____ , no matter how _____
                       PLURAL NOUN   ADJECTIVE

  or small they are.

- Surround yourself with _____ who support and encourage
                           PLURAL NOUN

  you! My biggest fan happens to be a tiny but _____ dragon—
                                                  ADJECTIVE

  not your common best _____ , I know.
                          NOUN

So are you ready to find your inner _____? You can do it!
                                       NOUN

From DISNEY PRINCESS MAD LIBS® • Copyright © 2019 Disney Enterprises, Inc. All rights reserved.
Published by Mad Libs, an imprint of Penguin Random House LLC.

MAD LIBS® is fun to play with friends, but you can also play it by yourself! To begin with, DO NOT look at the story on the page below. Fill in the blanks on this page with the words called for. Then, using the words you have selected, fill in the blank spaces in the story.

Now you've created your own hilarious MAD LIBS® game!

ADVICE FROM POCAHONTAS

PLURAL NOUN _____

VERB _____

NOUN _____

ADJECTIVE _____

VERB _____

ADJECTIVE _____

VERB _____

NOUN _____

NOUN _____

PLURAL NOUN _____

NOUN _____

PART OF THE BODY _____

SAME PART OF THE BODY _____

VERB _____

NOUN _____

VERB _____

PLURAL NOUN _____

ADJECTIVE _____

VERB _____

MAD LIBS

ADVICE FROM POCAHONTAS

In your life, there will always be _____ telling you what they
PLURAL NOUN

think is best. It may not always be easy to _____ yourself, but
VERB

remember to always follow your own _____. It's important
NOUN

to be _____ and stand up for what you _____.
ADJECTIVE   VERB

Sometimes, doing the _____ thing means that people might
ADJECTIVE

_____ you. But if you are true to yourself, you will be at peace
VERB

with the _____. March to the beat of your own _____.
NOUN   NOUN

Your life is your own and you should make _____ that are
PLURAL NOUN

best for you. Sometimes you might need advice from your friends or

_____. Grandmother Willow's advice reminds us to listen with our
NOUN

_____. She knows that sometimes the _____
PART OF THE BODY   SAME PART OF THE BODY

and mind might _____, but being logical isn't always right. I can
VERB

always trust Grandmother _____'s advice because she has lots
NOUN

of experience to _____. Her _____ of wisdom are
VERB   PLURAL NOUN

always _____. So remember: Be like a river and _____
ADJECTIVE   VERB

your own path!

From DISNEY PRINCESS MAD LIBS® • Copyright © 2019 Disney Enterprises, Inc. All rights reserved.
Published by Mad Libs, an imprint of Penguin Random House LLC.

MAD LIBS® is fun to play with friends, but you can also play it by yourself! To begin with, DO NOT look at the story on the page below. Fill in the blanks on this page with the words called for. Then, using the words you have selected, fill in the blank spaces in the story.

Now you've created your own hilarious MAD LIBS® game!

MAKE A WISH WITH TIANA

VERB _____

ADJECTIVE _____

NOUN _____

PART OF THE BODY (PLURAL) _____

NOUN _____

NOUN _____

PART OF THE BODY (PLURAL) _____

NOUN _____

VERB ENDING IN "ING" _____

VERB (PAST TENSE) _____

NOUN _____

VERB _____

PART OF THE BODY _____

PLURAL NOUN _____

ADJECTIVE _____

NOUN _____

Is there a wish you want to _____ with all your heart? It only
                                    VERB

takes a few _____ steps.
                 ADJECTIVE

- First, find a/an _____ with a great view of the starry sky.
                      NOUN

- Next, close your _____ and focus on your _____ .
                    PART OF THE BODY (PLURAL)   NOUN

- Now that you've thought of your _____ , open your
                                      NOUN

  _____ and look for the brightest _____ in the
  PART OF THE BODY (PLURAL)   NOUN

  night sky. It's even more magical to spot a/an _____ star!
                                                 VERB ENDING IN "ING"

- When you've _____ your star, it's time to make your
                VERB (PAST TENSE)

  _____ .
      NOUN

- _____ your wish and remember to believe in it with all your
     VERB

  _____ .
  PART OF THE BODY

Wishing on _____ is enchanting, but it really takes _____
           PLURAL NOUN   ADJECTIVE

work, love, and determination to make your _____ come true.
                                                NOUN

From DISNEY PRINCESS MAD LIBS® • Copyright © 2019 Disney Enterprises, Inc. All rights reserved.
Published by Mad Libs, an imprint of Penguin Random House LLC.

MAD LIBS® is fun to play with friends, but you can also play it by yourself! To begin with, DO NOT look at the story on the page below. Fill in the blanks on this page with the words called for. Then, using the words you have selected, fill in the blank spaces in the story.

Now you've created your own hilarious MAD LIBS® game!

RAPUNZEL'S READY FOR THE WORLD

ADJECTIVE _____

VERB _____

NOUN _____

PLURAL NOUN _____

VERB _____

PERSON IN ROOM _____

NOUN _____

TYPE OF LIQUID _____

TYPE OF FOOD (PLURAL) _____

NOUN _____

VERB _____

NOUN _____

VERB _____

PLURAL NOUN _____

ADJECTIVE _____

VERB _____

ADJECTIVE _____

VERB ENDING IN "ING" _____

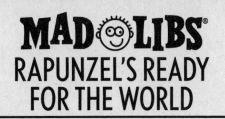

So long, _____ tower, I'm ready to _____! There is a
               ADJECTIVE   VERB

huge _____ out there, and there are so many _____
            NOUN   PLURAL NOUN

I'm ready to visit. I would love to _____ Prague and see
                                              VERB

the beautiful church of St. _____ and Old Town Hall's
                                  PERSON IN ROOM

astronomical _____. Imagine if I made it to Vienna—I would sip
                    NOUN

_____ and eat delicious _____ till I couldn't
TYPE OF LIQUID   TYPE OF FOOD (PLURAL)

eat another bite! I could even sail on a/an _____ down the Danube
                                                   NOUN

River to Bratislava, where I would _____ through Devin Castle
                                           VERB

with its beautiful _____ Tower. After that, I would visit Warsaw,
                          NOUN

of course, where I'd _____ the cobbled _____ of the
                            VERB   PLURAL NOUN

Old Town Square. There are so many _____ things to do, where do
                                          ADJECTIVE

I start? Oh, I know! More than anything, I can't wait to see the golden lights

that _____ every year on my birthday. They make my birthday feel
            VERB

so _____, like they're _____ just for me.
      ADJECTIVE   VERB ENDING IN "ING"

From DISNEY PRINCESS MAD LIBS® • Copyright © 2019 Disney Enterprises, Inc. All rights reserved.
Published by Mad Libs, an imprint of Penguin Random House LLC.

MAD LIBS® is fun to play with friends, but you can also play it by yourself! To begin with, DO NOT look at the story on the page below. Fill in the blanks on this page with the words called for. Then, using the words you have selected, fill in the blank spaces in the story.

Now you've created your own hilarious MAD LIBS® game!

AURORA'S SWEET SIXTEEN!

NUMBER _____

NOUN _____

PLURAL NOUN _____

NOUN _____

VERB ENDING IN "ING" _____

PLURAL NOUN _____

ADJECTIVE _____

PART OF THE BODY (PLURAL) _____

VERB _____

ANIMAL (PLURAL) _____

ADJECTIVE _____

ADJECTIVE _____

ADJECTIVE _____

NOUN _____

VERB _____

ADJECTIVE _____

MAD LIBS®
AURORA'S SWEET SIXTEEN!

I can't wait for my birthday! I'll finally be _____ years old. That means

NUMBER

I'll be a young _____ who can make her own _____ .

NOUN   PLURAL NOUN

Best of all, my aunties will treat me like a/an _____ ! For my

NOUN

birthday there will be lots of _____ and dancing among

VERB ENDING IN "ING"

the _____ in the forest. It will be so _____ to

PLURAL NOUN   ADJECTIVE

dance in bare feet and feel the grass between my _____ .

PART OF THE BODY (PLURAL)

All my friends who _____ in the forest will be party

VERB

guests—the chirping birds, the chattering _____ , and the

ANIMAL (PLURAL)

_____ rabbits. And, of course, it's not a birthday without a

ADJECTIVE

beautiful and _____ cake. And how _____ would it

ADJECTIVE   ADJECTIVE

be if the handsome _____ I dreamed about last night came to my

NOUN

party? We would sing and spin around as we _____ . This will

VERB

certainly be the most _____ birthday ever!

ADJECTIVE

From DISNEY PRINCESS MAD LIBS® • Copyright © 2019 Disney Enterprises, Inc. All rights reserved.
Published by Mad Libs, an imprint of Penguin Random House LLC.

Download Mad Libs today!

Join the millions of Mad Libs fans
creating wacky and wonderful
stories on our apps!

©Disney